LOVE V

. . . .

The Ultimate Vegan Mug Cake Cookbook

Zoe Hazan

 HIGH CEDAR PRESS

LOVE VEGAN

The Ultimate Vegan Mug Cake Cookbook

High Cedar Press

Copyright © 2017

Kindle Edition

DISCLAIMER

TThe full contents of 'Love Vegan', including text, comments, graphics, images, and other content are for informational purposes only. The information is not intended to diagnose, treat, cure or prevent any illnesses or diseases. Always consult you physician before changing dietary habits.

'Love Vegan' does not provide specific information or advice regarding food intolerance or allergies. It is the responsibility of the reader to ensure any diagnosed or potential food intolerances are identified and excluded from the recipes.

The author and publisher make no guarantee as to the availability of ingredients mentioned in this book. Many ingredients vary in size and texture and these differences may affect the outcome of some recipes. The author has tried to make the recipes as accurate and workable as possible, however, cannot be responsible for any recipe not working.

Every effort has been made to prepare this material to ensure it's accuracy, however, the author nor publisher will be held responsible if there is information deemed as inaccurate.

CONTENTS

Introduction   6
Mug Cake Basics   7
Ingredients   8
Tips and Troubleshooting   10

MUG CAKES

Cookie Dough   12
Peanut Butter Cake   13
Cinnamon Roll   14
Vanilla Chai   15
Vanilla Cake   16
Red Velvet   18
Gooey S'mores Cake   19
Pancakes in a Mug   21
Tiramisu   22
Mocha Cake   24
Coffee Cake   26
Mug Pound Cake   27
Gingerbread Mug Cake with Cranberry Compote   28
Cinnamon & Raisin English Muffin   30
Funfetti Cake with Vanilla Strawberry Ice Cream   32

CHOCOLATE

Chocolate Brownie   35
Chocolate Raspberry Lava Cake   36
Chocolate Chip Espresso   37
Chocolate Matcha Cake   38
Chocolate Chip Banana Muffins   39
Creamy Chocolate Pudding   40
Chocolate Hazelnut Mug Cake   41
Walnut Brownie Sundae   42
Mint Chocolate Chip   43
Chocolate Strawberry Cake   44

FRUITY

Blueberry Muffin   46
Apple Cinnamon Crumble   48
Salted Caramel & Apple   50
Moist Carrot Cake   51
Pumpkin Pie   52
Sticky Date Pudding   53
Coconut Cake   54
Sweet Avocado & Coconut   55
Mango Coconut Cake   56
Pear & Almond   57
Banana Nut Crunch   59
Peanut Butter & Banana Oatmeal   60
Pineapple Upside Down Mug Cake   61
Raspberry Almond Cake   62
Spiced Sweet Potato Mug Cake   64
Lemon Mug Cake with Lemon Drizzle   66

Toppings

Salted Caramel Sauce   69
Chocolate Chips   71
Coconut Cream Topping   72
Preview of 'The Essential Mexican Cookbook for Vegans'
Including a FREE recipe!   73
Avocado Enchiladas   74

INTRODUCTION

There is something so soothing about cradling a warm mug in the palm of your hands, absorb the warmth and slide your fingers towards the handle while having a break or a quick exchange with a friend or a colleague. Now imagine that the content of the mug is not liquid but one of your favorite cake! Heaven, or as we call it...a Mug Cake!

The beauty of Mug Cakes is their universality. They suit all kinds of diets. Perfect for vegans, vegetarians and indeed everyone else who fancies a mug of deliciousness. Their overwhelming advantage is the time they take to make: no more than 5 minutes in the microwave.

The ingredients are simple and easy to source, as a matter of fact, you probably already have the basic ingredients in your pantry. The difficulty will probably be to decide which recipe to prepare!

MUG CAKE BASICS

THE MUG

Although there are many commercial cups specifically designed for mug cakes, some of which are very attractive indeed, there is no need for a specific container. Any ceramic mug will do a great job, as long as is it microwave proof. The ideal size is 400 ml, as it leaves enough room for all the ingredients and allows the cake to rise.

THE MICROWAVE

Who would have thought that you could mix some basic ingredients in a mug, throw it in the microwave for a few minutes and be presented with a deliciously moist and yummy cake!

It goes without saying that all microwaves heat differently. This means you may need a little trial and error to get it right, but believe us when we say it will be so worth it!

The timings in this cookbook are simply a guide, but you may find you will need to alter the cooking time when making your mug cake at home. Our best advice is to keep a close eye on your cake. If the cake seems too dry, give it 10-20 seconds less next time you make a cake, or if it is too wet, pop it back in the micro and heat for 10-20 seconds more.

INGREDIENTS

Non-Dairy Milks

All the recipes in this book privilege ingredients beneficial to your health such as non-dairy milk. These are now readily available in supermarkets, due to the increasing number of people sensitive to cow or goat milk, but also, because non-dairy milk has intrinsic advantages.

For example, almond milk contains no cholesterol or saturated fat, it's high in healthy fats (such as omega fatty acids, typically found in fish), which helps to prevent high blood pressure and heart disease.

For our 'Love Vegan' mug cake recipes, we have used ingredients suitable for vegans, vegetarians as well as health conscious individuals. You should consider replacing dairy milk with almond, soy, and coconut milk if you are looking to improve your diet.

Choice of Flour

Flour is often something we take for granted. A tasteless ingredient which we tend to oversee. Flour is flour. Well, not exactly. Each type of flour you use has a unique composition and baking properties. Keep in mind it's never a good idea to substitute flours.

Coconut flour, for example, because it's not a grain-based flour, is very low in carbohydrates and high in fibers. You will find that the recipes using coconut flour call for about half the amount of traditional flour, this is because a tablespoon only will go a long way.

Sweeteners

We all know that when baking a cake or a batch of cookies you cannot play around with the measurements of ingredients. Everything has to be accurate or you will end up with an inedible mess! Mug cakes are a whole different story! Although we would not recommend altering the flour and milk (dry and liquid) ingredients, you can play around with the sweeteners as well as the toppings.

The options are endless when it comes to how you wish to sweeten your mug cake. Do you prefer the warm caramel hint from brown sugar, or perhaps the subtle sweetness from a drop of agave nectar? This is an element that you can alter, so although many of the recipes call for sugar, keep in mind you can substitute your favorite sweetener and add it according to your taste.

Measurements

Mug cakes are very quick and easy to prepare. No need for smart electronic kitchen gadgets - a good old tablespoon is all you'll need. But if you prefer weighing the ingredients, 1 tbsp of flour is the equivalent of 8 grams and 1 tbsp milk equals 15ml.

TIPS AND TROUBLESHOOTING

Making the perfect mug cake tends to require a little trial and error as there are many varying factors, for example, the type of ingredients you use, the heat of your microwave and the mug you use. Trust us, once you have made a few cakes at home, you will become a pro!

Here are a few tips and tricks we have learned along the way to help get you started.

• Like any other dish, the inside of the mugs will need to be greased before use. You can use a little butter, but for the vegan diet, we recommend an oil such as coconut, vegetable or canola.

• Avoid opening the microwave while the mug is bubbling. A plate or paper towel will catch any overflow.

• We like to protect our microwave and minimize cleaning by placing a plate or a paper towel on the microwave plate, just in case the mixture overflows.

• To prevent over-working the mixture, mix all the wet ingredients first and add the flour last.

• You can choose to replace sugar with healthier options such as maple syrup or honey though the latter might not be an option for vegans.

• Last but not least where our mug cakes recipes recommend a topping, follow the instructions or let your creativity flow and see where it leads you.

• Mug cakes truly are the perfect treat when you are craving something a little sweet, without the need to bake an entire cake or a batch of cookies.

So what are you waiting for? Grab your favorite mug and try one of these easy and delicious recipes, and within 5 minutes you will have a wonderful mug cake ready to be devoured!

MUG CAKES

COOKIE DOUGH

Preparation Time
3 minutes

Total Time
4 minutes

Makes
1 serving

INGREDIENTS

1 small ripe mashed banana
1 ½ tbsp almond butter
½ tsp vanilla extract
1 tbsp coconut milk
1 tbsp coconut flour
½ tsp baking powder
½ tbsp brown sugar
¼ tsp ground cinnamon
Pinch of salt
1 tbsp cacao nibs

DIRECTIONS

Grease a medium-large mug with a little coconut or vegetable oil.

In a small bowl mix together flour, baking powder, sugar, cinnamon and salt.

In a separate small bowl add mashed banana, nut butter, vanilla, and coconut milk, and mix well.

Combine flour mixture with banana mixture and whisk well until a lump-free batter is formed. Fold in cacao nibs.

Pour into greased mug.

Microwave on high for around 90 seconds or until the cake has risen and it springs back when you poke it. If it is not fully cooked microwave it for a further 10 seconds until a toothpick comes out clean.

PEANUT BUTTER CAKE

Preparation Time
2 minutes

Total Time
3 minutes

Makes
1 serving

INGREDIENTS

2 tbsp all-purpose flour
¼ tsp baking powder
Pinch of salt
2 tbsp peanut butter
2 tbsp unsweetened non-dairy milk
1 tbsp maple syrup
1 tsp vanilla extract
Vegan chocolate chips to garnish, see recipe

DIRECTIONS

Grease a medium-large mug with a little coconut or vegetable oil.

In a small bowl combine flour, salt, and baking powder. In a separate small bowl whisk together peanut butter, non-dairy milk, maple syrup and vanilla extract.

Pour flour mixture and peanut mixture into the mug and whisk well until a smooth batter is formed.

Microwave on high for around 60 seconds or until the cake has risen and it springs back when you poke it. If it is not fully cooked microwave it for a further 20 seconds until a toothpick comes out clean.

Top with chocolate chips if using and serve immediately.

CINNAMON ROLL

Preparation Time
2 minutes

Total Time
3 minutes

Makes
1 serving

INGREDIENTS

2 tbsp all-purpose flour
¼ tsp baking powder
Pinch of salt
2 tbsp unsweetened non-dairy milk
1 tbsp maple syrup or brown sugar
½ tsp vanilla extract
1 tsp coconut oil, melted

FOR THE TOPPING

1 tbsp brown sugar
¼ tsp ground cinnamon

DIRECTIONS

Grease a medium-large mug with a little coconut or vegetable oil.

In a small bowl combine flour, baking powder, salt, milk, maple syrup/sugar, vanilla and coconut oil until a smooth batter is formed. Pour into greased mug and set aside.

In a separate bowl combine brown sugar and cinnamon and pour on top of mug cake.

Microwave on high for around 60 seconds or until the cake has risen and it springs back when you poke it. If it is not fully cooked microwave it for a further 20 seconds until a toothpick comes out clean.

VANILLA CHAI

Preparation Time
3 minutes (+ a few
minutes for tea
bag to steep)

Total Time
4 minutes

Makes
1 serving

INGREDIENTS

2 tbsp all-purpose flour
¼ tsp baking powder
1 ½ tbsp granulated sugar
Pinch of salt
2 ½ tbsp dairy free milk
¾ tbsp coconut oil
½ tsp vanilla extract

Chai tea bag (you can use
a flavored tea bag such as
vanilla)

DIRECTIONS

Pour milk into a microwave-safe bowl and heat for 40 seconds.
Place chai tea bag into warm milk and steep for a few minutes
while you prepare the other ingredients.

Grease a medium-large mug with a little coconut or vegetable
oil.

In a small bowl mix together flour, baking powder, sugar, and
salt.

Using a teaspoon press the tea bag against the side or bottom
of the mug to release as much flavor as possible. Remove and
discard tea bag.

Add coconut oil and vanilla extract to the milk and stir. Combine
flour mixture with chai milk mixture and whisk well.

Pour into greased mug and microwave for 1 minute and 10
seconds or until a toothpick comes out clean.

VANILLA CAKE

Preparation Time
2 minutes
(+ 15 minutes for
flax egg to set in
the fridge)

Total Time
3 minutes

Makes
1 serving

INGREDIENTS

1 tbsp ground flax seeds + 3 tbsp water
1 ½ tbsp coconut flour
1 tbsp almond flour
Pinch of salt
¼ tsp cinnamon powder
½ tsp baking powder
1 tbsp granulated sugar
1 tsp vanilla extract
3 tbsp unsweetened non-dairy milk

DIRECTIONS

In a small bowl combine 1 tablespoon of ground flax seeds or chia seeds with 3 tablespoons of water and transfer to the fridge for 15 minutes.

Grease a medium-large mug with a little coconut or vegetable oil.

In a small bowl combine coconut and almond flour, salt, cinnamon, baking powder, and sugar. Set aside until the flax/chia mixture has set.

Add vanilla and non-dairy milk to the flax/chia mixture and pour into dry mixture. Whisk well, adding another tablespoon of non-dairy milk if the mixture seems too dry.

Pour into greased mug and microwave on high for around 60 seconds or until the cake has risen and it springs back when you poke it. If it is not fully cooked microwave it for a further 20 seconds until a toothpick comes out clean.

RED VELVET

Preparation Time
3 minutes

Total Time
4 minutes

Makes
1 serving

INGREDIENTS

3 tbsp all-purpose flour
2 heaped tbsp sugar
2 tsp unsweetened cocoa
¼ tsp baking powder
Pinch of baking soda
Pinch of salt
1 tbsp melted coconut oil
2 tbsp + 2 tsp dairy free milk
⅛ tsp apple cider vinegar
1 tsp vegan red food coloring
(optional)
½ tsp vanilla

DIRECTIONS

Grease a medium-large mug with a little coconut or vegetable oil.

In a small bowl combine flour, sugar, cocoa, baking powder, baking soda, and salt.

In a separate small bowl combine oil, milk, vinegar, food coloring and vanilla.

Combine the wet and dry ingredients and whisk well until there are no lumps and a smooth batter is formed. Pour into greased mug.

Microwave on high for around 90 seconds or until the cake has risen and it springs back when you poke it. If it is not fully cooked microwave it for a further 20 seconds until a toothpick comes out clean.

GOOEY S'MORES CAKE

Preparation Time
4 minutes

Total Time
5 minutes

Makes
1 serving

INGREDIENTS

2 cinnamon graham cracker sheets or 1 McVitie's Ginger Nut*

5 tbsp dairy free milk, divided

2 tsp maple syrup

⅛ tsp ground cinnamon

3 tbsp all-purpose flour

1 tbsp cocoa powder

1 tbsp brown sugar

Pinch of salt

½ tsp vanilla extract

3 vegan marshmallows, chopped in half

1 tbsp vegan chocolate chips

*At the time of print Graham Crackers and McVitie's Ginger Nuts are vegan, however, manufacturers are at liberty to change their ingredients at any time. Please check the ingredients before using.

DIRECTIONS

In a small bowl crumble the graham crackers/ginger nuts until it resembles a coarse meal. Remove 1 tbsp and set aside.

Grease a medium-large mug with a little oil.

Add 2 tbsp milk, 1 tsp maple syrup and cinnamon to the graham cracker crumbs, mixing well, and push firmly into the base and sides of the mug. Set aside.

In a separate bowl combine flour, cocoa powder, sugar, salt, vanilla, remaining milk and remaining maple syrup. Fold in chocolate chips.

Add 1 marshmallow (two halves) to the bottom of the mug, then pour batter over the top.

Sprinkle 1 tbsp of remaining graham cracker crumbs over then top them place two marshmallows on the surface.

Microwave on high for 1 minute and 30 seconds or until the cake has risen. If it is not fully cooked microwave it for a further 10 seconds until a toothpick comes out clean.

PANCAKES IN A MUG

Preparation Time	Total Time	Makes
3 minutes	4 minutes	1 serving

INGREDIENTS

¼ cup all-purpose flour
1 tbsp granulated sugar
½ tsp baking powder
Pinch of salt
2 tbsp dairy free milk
1 tbsp vegan butter, melted
2 ½ tbsp applesauce
½ tsp vanilla extract
Maple syrup to drizzle on top

DIRECTIONS

Grease a medium-large mug with a little coconut or vegetable oil.

In a small bowl combine flour, sugar, salt, and baking powder.

In a separate bowl combine milk, melted butter, applesauce and vanilla extract and stir.

Combine wet and dry ingredients and whisk until a smooth batter is formed.

Pour into greased mug.

Microwave on high for around 1 minute and 30 seconds or until the cake has risen and it springs back when you poke it. If it is not fully cooked microwave it for a further 10 seconds until a toothpick comes out clean.

Drizzle with maple syrup and serve immediately.

TIRAMISU

Preparation Time
3 minutes
(+ 15 mins for 'flax
egg' to set)

Total Time
4 minutes

Makes
1 serving

INGREDIENTS

FOR THE CAKE:

1 tbsp ground flax seeds + 3 tbsp water
1 ½ tbsp coconut flour
1 tbsp almond flour
1 tsp unsweetened cocoa powder
½ tsp espresso powder
pinch of salt
½ tsp baking powder
1 tbsp brown sugar or maple syrup

½ tsp vanilla extract
1 tbsp coconut cream
2 tbsp dairy free milk

FOR THE 'TIRAMISU' TOPPING:

1 tsp unsweetened cocoa powder
1 tsp brown sugar or sweetener of choice
¼ tsp cinnamon powder

DIRECTIONS

In a small bowl combine 1 tablespoon of ground flax seeds with 3 tablespoons of water and transfer to the fridge for 15 minutes.

Grease a medium-large mug with a little coconut or vegetable oil.

In a small bowl combine both flours, cocoa powder, espresso powder, salt, baking powder, and sugar. If using maple syrup add it to the bowl of wet ingredients in the next step.

Remove the flax mixture from the fridge and add vanilla, coconut cream and dairy free milk (and maple syrup if using in replace of sugar). Whisk wet and dry ingredients together until a smooth batter is formed. Pour into greased mug.

Combine topping ingredients and sprinkle over mug cake.

Microwave on high for around 1 minute or until the cake has risen and it springs back when you poke it. If it is not fully cooked microwave it for a further 10 seconds until a toothpick comes out clean.

MOCHA CAKE

Preparation Time
2 minutes
(+ 15 minutes for
flax egg to set)

Total Time
4 minutes

Makes
1 serving

INGREDIENTS

1 tbsp flax seeds + 3 tbsp water
2 tbsp + 2 tsp flour
2 tbsp brown sugar
1 tbsp cocoa powder
Pinch of salt
½ tsp baking powder
1 tsp granulated coffee
2 tbsp dairy free milk
2 tbsp vegan butter, melted
½ tsp vanilla extract
2 tbsp vegan chocolate chips, divided
2 tsp of water, divided

DIRECTIONS

In a small bowl combine 1 tablespoon of ground flaxseed with 3 tablespoons of water and transfer to the fridge for 15 minutes.

Grease a medium-large mug with a little coconut oil.

In a small bowl combine flour, sugar, cocoa powder, salt, baking powder, and coffee.

In a separate bowl combine milk, vegan butter, vanilla extract and flaxseed mixture.

Combine wet and dry ingredients and whisk until a smooth batter is formed then fold in 1 tbsp chocolate chips.

Pour 1 more tbsp chocolate chips on top of the cake batter, allowing them to rest on the surface. Add 1 tbsp water to the surface of the batter, on top of the chocolate chips.

Microwave on high for around 1 minute and 30 seconds or until the cake has risen and it springs back when you poke it. If it is not fully cooked microwave it for a further 10 seconds until a toothpick comes out clean.

COFFEE CAKE

Preparation Time
2 minutes

Total Time
3 minutes

Makes
1 serving

INGREDIENTS

2 tbsp all-purpose flour
¼ tsp baking powder
Pinch of salt
1 tbsp brown sugar
½ - ¾ tsp instant coffee powder
1 tbsp plus 2 tsp water
2 tsp oil or applesauce

½ tsp vanilla extract

For the Topping
¼ tsp cinnamon
1 ¼ tsp brown sugar
½ tsp oil
2 tsp crushed nuts (pecans or walnuts work well)

DIRECTIONS

Grease a medium-large mug with a little coconut or vegetable oil.

In a small bowl combine flour, baking powder, salt, sugar, coffee, water, oil/applesauce, and vanilla and whisk well until there are no lumps and a smooth batter is formed. Pour into greased mug.

In a separate small bowl combine cinnamon, sugar and oil, and mix well. Pour on top of mug cake.

Microwave on high for around 60 seconds or until the cake has risen and it springs back when you poke it. If it is not fully cooked microwave it for a further 20 seconds until a toothpick comes out clean.

Top with crushed nuts and serve immediately while hot.

MUG POUND CAKE

Preparation Time
3 minutes

Total Time
4 minutes

Makes
1 serving

INGREDIENTS

1 tsp ground flax seeds
5 tbsp coconut flour
⅛ tsp baking powder
2 tbsp granulated sugar
1 tsp maple syrup
½ tsp vanilla extract
3 tbsp coconut oil (melted) or
vegetable oil
½ tsp ground cinnamon
½ tsp brown sugar

DIRECTIONS

Grease a medium-large mug with a little oil.

Combine flax seeds, coconut flour, baking powder, and sugar.

In a separate bowl combine syrup, vanilla and oil.

Gently add dry ingredients to the wet ingredients.

Pour into the mug and microwave on high for 2 minutes or until the cake has risen and it springs back when you poke it. If it is not fully cooked microwave it for a further 10 seconds until a toothpick comes out clean.

Wait 1-2 minutes for the cake to cool down then use a knife to release then turn upside down on a plate. Sprinkle with cinnamon and brown sugar.

GINGERBREAD MUG CAKE WITH CRANBERRY COMPOTE

Preparation Time
2 minutes

Total Time
4 minutes

Makes
1 serving

INGREDIENTS

FOR THE GINGERBREAD
MUG CAKE:

2 tbsp all-purpose
2 tbsp coconut flour
1 tbsp brown sugar
Pinch salt
1 tsp gingerbread spice
¼ tsp cinnamon powder
½ tsp baking powder
⅛ tsp baking soda
¼ cup + 1 tbsp dairy-free milk

2 tbsp unsweetened
applesauce
½ tsp vanilla extract

FOR THE CRANBERRY
COMPOTE:

¼ cup cranberries, fresh or
frozen
1 ½ tsp sugar

DIRECTIONS

Grease a medium-large mug with a little coconut oil.

In a small bowl combine both flours, sugar, salt, gingerbread spice, cinnamon, baking powder, and baking soda.

In a separate bowl combine milk, vanilla extract and applesauce.

Combine wet and dry ingredients and whisk until a smooth batter is formed.

Pour into the mug and microwave on high for around 1 minute and 30 seconds or until the cake has risen and it springs back when you poke it. If it is not fully cooked microwave it for a further 10 seconds until a toothpick comes out clean. Leave to cool for 2-3 minutes before serving.

FOR THE CRANBERRY COMPOTE:

Place cranberries in a small bowl and microwave on high for 45 seconds with 1 tbsp water.

Remove from microwave and stir in sugar.

Pour cranberry compote on top of gingerbread mug cake.

CINNAMON & RAISIN ENGLISH MUFFIN

Preparation Time
3 minutes
(+ 15 minutes for
flax egg to set)

Total Time
4 minutes

Makes
1 serving

INGREDIENTS

1 tbsp ground flax seeds + 3 tbsp water
2 tbsp almond flour
½ tsp baking powder
½ tsp cinnamon
Pinch of salt
2 tbsp applesauce
2 tbsp non-dairy milk
1 tsp vanilla extract
1 ½ tbsp raisins

DIRECTIONS

In a small bowl combine 1 tablespoon of ground flaxseed or chia seeds with 3 tablespoons of water and transfer to the fridge for 15 minutes.

Grease a medium-large mug with a little oil.

In a small bowl combine almond flour, baking powder, salt, and cinnamon and mix well.

In a separate bowl combine applesauce, milk, vanilla extract and the flax seed mixture.

Mix dry ingredients into wet and stir until fully combined.

Fold in raisins.

Pour into the mug and microwave on high for around 2 minutes or until the cake has risen and it springs back when you poke it. If it is not fully cooked microwave it for a further 10 seconds until a toothpick comes out clean.

Leave to cool, remove from the mug, then slice and toast for a few minutes on each side.

FUNFETTI CAKE WITH VANILLA STRAWBERRY ICE CREAM

Preparation Time
3 minutes
(+ 2 hours for the
ice cream to set)

Total Time
4 minutes

Makes
1 serving

INGREDIENTS

FOR THE MUG CAKE:

¼ cup all-purpose flour
2 ½ tbsp granulated sugar
½ tsp baking powder
Pinch of salt
¼ cup non-dairy milk
1 ½ tbsp melted coconut oil
½ tsp vanilla extract
½ tbsp sprinkles

FOR THE VANILLA STRAWBERRY ICE CREAM:

¼ cup coconut milk
3 tbsp mashed strawberries
1 tsp vanilla extract
1 tbsp powdered sugar

DIRECTIONS

FOR THE MUG CAKE:

Grease a medium-large mug with a little coconut or vegetable oil.

In a small bowl combine flour, sugar, baking powder, and salt.

In a separate small bowl combine milk, oil, and vanilla.

Combine wet and dry ingredients and whisk well until there are no lumps and a smooth batter is formed. Fold in sprinkles, saving some to sprinkle over the top. Pour into greased mug.

Microwave on high for around 60 seconds or until the cake has risen and it springs back when you poke it. If it is not fully cooked microwave it for a further 20 seconds until a toothpick comes out clean.

FOR THE STRAWBERRY ICE CREAM:

Whisk all ingredients together in a small bowl, cover with cling film and freeze for 1-2 hours.

Scoop on top of mug cake and serve immediately.

CHOCOLATE

CHOCOLATE BROWNIE

Preparation Time
2 minutes

Total Time
3 minutes

Makes
1 serving

INGREDIENTS

2 tbsp all purpose flour
1 tbsp brown sugar or maple syrup
2 tbsp unsweetened cocoa
¼ tsp cinnamon powder
½ tsp vanilla extract
Pinch of salt
3 tbsp coconut milk
1 tbsp melted coconut oil
1 tbsp vegan chocolate chips

DIRECTIONS

Grease a medium-large mug with a little coconut or vegetable oil.

In a small bowl combine flour, sugar/syrup, cocoa, cinnamon, vanilla, salt, coconut milk and oil and whisk well until there are no lumps and a smooth batter is formed.

Fold in chocolate chips

Pour into greased mug and microwave on high for around 60 seconds or until the cake has risen and it springs back when you poke it. If it is not fully cooked microwave it for a further 20 seconds until a toothpick comes out clean.

CHOCOLATE RASPBERRY LAVA CAKE

Preparation Time
3 minutes

Total Time
4 minutes

Makes
1 serving

INGREDIENTS

3 tbsp all-purpose flour
1 tbsp + 1 tsp cocoa powder
Pinch of salt
¼ tsp baking powder
1 tbsp sugar
⅛ tsp instant coffee granules
½ tsp vanilla extract

3 tbsp non-dairy milk
2 ½ tsp melted coconut oil
2 tbsp fresh raspberries, mashed
Handful vegan chocolate chips

DIRECTIONS

Grease a medium-large mug with a little coconut or vegetable oil.

In a small bowl mix together flour, cocoa powder, salt, baking powder, sugar, and coffee.

In a separate small bowl add vanilla, milk and oil, and mix well.

Combine flour mixture with milk mixture and whisk well until a lump-free batter is formed.

Pour half of the batter into the greased mug, top with raspberries and chocolate chips, then pour the remaining batter over.

Microwave on high for around 45 seconds or until the cake has risen and it springs back when you poke it. If it is not fully cooked microwave it for a further 10 seconds but do not overcook or the lava center will harden.

CHOCOLATE CHIP ESPRESSO

Preparation Time
3 minutes

Total Time
4 minutes

Makes
1 serving

INGREDIENTS

2 tbsp all-purpose flour
2 tsp sugar
1 tsp espresso powder
2 tsp cocoa powder
¼ tsp baking powder
Pinch of salt

2 tbsp non-dairy milk
1 tbsp unsweetened
applesauce
½ tsp vanilla extract
1-2 tbsp vegan chocolate
chips

DIRECTIONS

Grease a medium-large mug with a little coconut or vegetable oil.

In a small bowl combine flour, sugar, espresso powder, cocoa powder, baking powder, and salt.

In a separate small bowl combine milk, applesauce and vanilla.

Combine wet and dry ingredients and whisk well until there are no lumps and a smooth batter is formed. Fold in chocolate chips, saving some to sprinkle over the top. Pour into greased mug.

Microwave on high for around 60 seconds or until the cake has risen and it springs back when you poke it. If it is not fully cooked microwave it for a further 20 seconds until a toothpick comes out clean.

CHOCOLATE MATCHA CAKE

Preparation Time
3 minutes

Total Time
4 minutes

Makes
1 serving

INGREDIENTS

4 tbsp all-purpose flour
3 tbsp sugar
1 ½ tsp matcha powder
1 tsp cocoa powder
¼ tsp baking powder
3 tbsp dairy free milk
1 tbsp melted coconut oil
½ tsp vanilla extract
¼ tsp almond extract
2 tbsp vegan chocolate chips

DIRECTIONS

Grease a medium-large mug with a little coconut or vegetable oil.

In a small bowl combine flour, sugar, matcha powder, cocoa powder, and baking powder.

Add milk, coconut oil, vanilla, and almond extract and stir. Combine wet and dry ingredients and whisk until a smooth batter is formed.

Fold in chocolate chips. Pour into greased mug.

Microwave on high for around 1 minute and 30 seconds or until the cake has risen and it springs back when you poke it. If it is not fully cooked microwave it for a further 10 seconds until a toothpick comes out clean.

CHOCOLATE CHIP BANANA MUFFINS

Preparation Time
1 minute

Total Time
3 minutes

Makes
1 serving

INGREDIENTS

2 ½ tbsp all purpose flour
1 tbsp brown sugar
Pinch of salt
¼ tsp baking powder
⅛ tsp baking soda
½ tbsp cocoa powder
¼ tsp cinnamon

1 tbsp melted coconut oil
1 tbsp dairy free milk
2 tbsp mashed ripe banana
½ tsp vanilla extract
1 ½ tbsp vegan chocolate chunks, optional

DIRECTIONS

Line a medium-large mug with a little parchment paper.

In a small bowl combine flour, sugar, salt, baking powder, baking soda, cocoa powder, and cinnamon.

In a separate bowl combine milk, oil, mashed banana and vanilla extract and stir.

Combine wet and dry ingredients and whisk until a smooth batter is formed then fold in chocolate chunks.

Microwave on high for around 1 minute or until the cake has risen and it springs back when you poke it. If it is not fully cooked microwave it for a further 10 seconds until a toothpick comes out clean.

Cool for 2 minutes before serving.

CREAMY CHOCOLATE PUDDING

Preparation Time
1 minutes*

Total Time
3 minutes
(+ 1 hour to chill in
the fridge)

Makes
1 serving

INGREDIENTS

1 tbsp cornflour
2 tbsp brown sugar
⅛ tsp salt
1 tbsp cocoa powder
¼ tsp cinnamon powder
½ cup coconut milk
½ tsp pure vanilla extract

DIRECTIONS

Grease a medium-large mug with a little coconut oil.

In a small bowl combine cornflour, sugar, salt, cocoa powder, and cinnamon.

Slowly pour in coconut milk, whisking constantly to break up any lumps. Add vanilla extract

Microwave on high for around 40 seconds then remove and give it a quick stir. Place back in the microwave for a further 40 seconds.

Cover and cool in the fridge for a minimum of 1 hour before serving.

CHOCOLATE HAZELNUT MUG CAKE

Preparation Time
2 minutes

Total Time
5 minutes
(+ 15 minutes for
flax egg to set)

Makes
1 serving

INGREDIENTS

1 tbsp ground flax seeds + 3 tbsp water
3 tbsp all-purpose flour
1 tbsp brown sugar
Pinch of salt
¼ tsp baking powder
1 tbsp cocoa powder

1 tbsp unsweetened applesauce
1½ tbsp melted coconut oil
3 tbsp dairy free milk
1½ tbsp roasted hazelnuts, chopped

DIRECTIONS

In a small bowl combine 1 tablespoon of ground flax seeds with 3 tablespoons of water and transfer to the fridge for 15 minutes.

Grease a medium-large mug with a little oil.

In a small bowl combine flour, sugar, salt, baking powder, and cocoa powder.

In a separate bowl combine applesauce, coconut oil, and milk.

Combine wet and dry ingredients and whisk until a smooth batter is formed. Remove flax seed mixture and stir into batter, then fold in chopped hazelnuts.

Microwave on high for around 1 minute and 30 seconds or until the cake has risen and it springs back when you poke it. If it is not fully cooked microwave it for a further 10 seconds until a toothpick comes out clean.

WALNUT BROWNIE SUNDAE

Preparation Time
2 minutes

Total Time
3 minutes

Makes
1 serving

INGREDIENTS

4 tbsp all purpose flour
2 tbsp cocoa powder
4 tbsp sugar
Pinch of salt
2 tbsp melted coconut oil
2 tbsp water
1 tbsp toasted walnuts,
chopped
Vegan Ice Cream

DIRECTIONS

Grease a medium-large mug with a little oil.

In a small bowl combine flour, cocoa powder, sugar, and salt and mix well.

Slowly add vegetable oil and water and whisk until a smooth batter is formed.

Fold in walnuts.

Pour into the mug and microwave on high for around 1 minute and 30 seconds or until the cake has risen and it springs back when you poke it. If it is not fully cooked microwave it for a further 10 seconds until a toothpick comes out clean. Leave to cool for 1 minute before serving.

Serve with a scoop of vegan ice cream.

MINT CHOCOLATE CHIP

| **Preparation Time** | **Total Time** | **Makes** |
| 2 minutes | 3 minutes | 1 serving |

INGREDIENTS

¼ cup oat flour
2 tbsp white sugar
Pinch of salt
½ tsp baking powder
1 ½ tsp melted coconut oil
2 tbsp non-dairy milk
¼ tsp mint extract
2 tbsp ripe avocado, mashed
1 tbsp vegan chocolate chips

DIRECTIONS

Grease a medium-large mug with a little oil.

In a small bowl combine flour, sugar, salt, and baking powder, and mix well.

Slowly add coconut oil, milk, mint extract and avocado and whisk until a smooth batter is formed.

Fold in chocolate chips.

Pour into the mug and microwave on high for around 1 minute and 30 seconds or until the cake has risen and it springs back when you poke it. If it is not fully cooked microwave it for a further 10 seconds until a toothpick comes out clean. Leave to cool for 1 minute before serving.

CHOCOLATE STRAWBERRY CAKE

Preparation Time
2 minutes

Total Time
3 minutes

Makes
1 serving

INGREDIENTS

1 tbsp all purpose flour
¼ tsp baking powder
1 tsp cocoa powder
2 tsp brown sugar
1 pinch salt
¼ tsp white vinegar
2 ½ tbsp warm water
2 tsp melted coconut oil
1 tbsp vegan strawberry jam
½ tsp vanilla extract

DIRECTIONS

Grease a medium-large mug with a little oil.

Combine flour, baking powder, cocoa powder, sugar, and salt.

In a separate bowl combine vinegar, water, oil, jam, and vanilla.

Slowly add wet ingredients into the dry ingredients and use a whisk to combine.

Pour into the mug and microwave on high for 1 minutes or until the cake has risen and it springs back when you poke it. If it is not fully cooked microwave it for a further 10 seconds until a toothpick comes out clean.

FRUITY

BLUEBERRY MUFFIN

Preparation Time
2 minutes
(+15 minutes for
the flax egg to set)

Total Time
3 minutes

Makes
1 serving

INGREDIENTS

1 tbsp ground flax seeds + 3 tbsp water
1 tbsp coconut flour
1 tbsp almond flour
1 tbsp all-purpose flour
2 tbsp granulated sugar
¼ tsp cinnamon
½ tsp baking powder
1 tbsp mashed banana (overripe bananas are best)
2 tbsp non-dairy milk
2 tbsp fresh or frozen blueberries

DIRECTIONS

In a small bowl combine 1 tablespoon of ground flax seed or chia seeds with 3 tablespoons of water and transfer to the fridge for 15 minutes.

Grease a medium-large mug with a little coconut or vegetable oil.

In a small bowl combine all flours, sugar, cinnamon and baking powder.

Once the flax/chia mixture has set remove it from the fridge and stir in mashed banana and milk.

Combine flax-banana mixture with flour mixture and whisk well until there are no lumps and a smooth batter is formed.

Gently fold in blueberries, then pour into greased mug.

Microwave on high for around 60 seconds or until the cake has risen and it springs back when you poke it. If it is not fully cooked microwave it for a further 20 seconds until a toothpick comes out clean.

APPLE CINNAMON CRUMBLE

Preparation Time
3 minutes

Total Time
4 minutes

Makes
1 serving

INGREDIENTS

FOR THE CRUMBLE TOPPING:

1 tbsp vegan butter
1 tbsp light brown sugar
1 tbsp old-fashioned rolled oats
1 tbsp all-purpose flour
½ tsp cinnamon
¼ tsp ground nutmeg
Pinch of salt

FOR THE APPLE BASE LAYER:

½ medium apple, chopped into ¼ -inch cubes
¼ tbsp vegan butter
1 tbsp light brown sugar
½ tbsp granulated sugar
½ tsp cornstarch
½ tsp cinnamon
¼ tsp ground nutmeg
½ tsp vanilla extract
Pinch of salt

DIRECTIONS

FOR THE CRUMBLE TOPPING:

Combine all ingredients using a fork until a coarse mixture is formed. You want this mixture to have texture. Set aside

For the Apple Base Layer:

Grease a medium-large mug with a little coconut or vegetable oil.

In a small microwave-safe bowl add chopped apple and butter. Microwave on high for 1 minute to soften the apples.

Remove from microwave and add both sugars, cornstarch, cinnamon, nutmeg, vanilla and salt, and stir to combine.

Pour into greased mug and top with crumble.

Microwave on high for around 1 minute and 20 seconds or until the top is bubbling and the cake has risen. If it is not fully cooked microwave for a further 20 seconds until a toothpick comes out clean.

SALTED CARAMEL & APPLE

Preparation Time
3 minutes

Total Time
4 minutes

Makes
1 serving

INGREDIENTS

2 tbsp apples, chopped into
¼-inch cubes
¼ cup all-purpose flour
2 ½ tbsp applesauce
1 tbsp sugar
1 tbsp non-dairy milk
¼ tsp baking powder
¼ tsp cinnamon powder
Pinch of salt
2 tbsp salted caramel sauce,
divided (see recipe)

DIRECTIONS

Grease a medium-large mug with a little coconut or vegetable oil.

In a small microwave-safe bowl add chopped apple. Microwave on high for 1 minute to soften the apples.

Remove from microwave and add flour, applesauce, sugar, milk, baking powder, cinnamon, salt, and 1 tablespoon of caramel sauce, stir to combine.

Pour mixture into greased mug and top with 1 tablespoon of caramel sauce.

Microwave on high for around 1 minute and 20 seconds or until the top is bubbling and the cake has risen. If it is not fully cooked microwave for a further 20 seconds until a toothpick comes out clean.

MOIST CARROT CAKE

Preparation Time	**Total Time**	**Makes**
3 minutes	4 minutes	1 serving

INGREDIENTS

2 heaped tbsp grated carrot
3 tbsp flour
2 tbsp brown sugar
¼ tsp cinnamon
¼ tsp baking powder
3 tbsp water
3 ½ tbsp melted coconut oil
¼ tsp vanilla extract
2 tbsp walnuts, roughly chopped

DIRECTIONS

Grease a medium-large mug with a little coconut or vegetable oil.

In a small microwave-safe bowl add grated carrot. Microwave on high for 40 seconds to soften.

Remove from microwave and add flour, brown sugar, cinnamon, baking powder, water, oil, and vanilla, stir to combine.

Pour mixture into greased mug.

Microwave on high for around 1 minute and 20 seconds or until the top is bubbling and the cake has risen. If it is not fully cooked microwave for a further 20 seconds until a toothpick comes out clean.

Top with chopped walnuts.

PUMPKIN PIE

Preparation Time
15 minutes

Total Time
30 minutes
(including 15
minutes for the
cookies to chill in
the fridge)

Makes
4-6 servings

INGREDIENTS

1 ½ tbs almond meal
¼ tsp baking powder
1 tsp pumpkin spice
¼ tsp ground cinnamon
2 tbsp + 2 tsp cup pumpkin puree

1 tbs coconut oil, melted
2 tbsp applesauce
1 tbsp + 1 tsp non-dairy milk
1 tsp vanilla essence
1 tbs maple syrup

DIRECTIONS

Grease a medium-large mug with a little coconut oil.

In a small bowl combine almond meal, baking powder, pumpkin spice and cinnamon.

In a separate bowl combine pumpkin puree, coconut oil, milk, applesauce, vanilla, and maple syrup.

Combine wet and dry ingredients and whisk until a smooth batter is formed.

Microwave on high for around 1 minute and 30 seconds or until the cake has risen and it springs back when you poke it. If it is not fully cooked microwave it for a further 10 seconds until a toothpick comes out clean.

STICKY DATE PUDDING

Preparation Time
3 minutes
(+15 minutes for
the flax egg to set)

Total Time
4 minutes

Makes
1 serving

INGREDIENTS

1 tsp ground flax seeds + 3 tsp water
3 tbsp all-purpose flour
¼ tsp baking powder
⅛ tsp baking soda
Pinch of salt
3 tbsp dairy free milk

1 tbsp + 1 tsp maple syrup, divided
1 ½ tbsp melted coconut oil
6 pitted dates, finely chopped

DIRECTIONS

Combine the flax seeds and water in a bowl and leave in fridge to set for 15 minutes

Grease a medium-large mug with a little oil.

Combine flour, baking powder, baking soda, and salt.

Add non-dairy milk, 1 tbsp maple syrup, oil, flax seed mixture and dates, and mix thoroughly using a whisk.

Pour into a mug and microwave on high for 1 minutes and 30 seconds or until the cake has risen and it springs back when you poke it. If it is not fully cooked microwave it for a further 10 seconds until a toothpick comes out clean.

Drizzle with 1 tsp maple syrup.

COCONUT CAKE

Preparation Time
2 minutes
(+15 minutes for
the flax egg to set)

Total Time
4 minutes

Makes
1 serving

INGREDIENTS

1 tbsp ground flax seeds + 3 tbsp water
1 tbsp all purpose flour
1 tbsp sugar
1 tbsp cocoa powder
1 tbsp desiccated coconut
1 tbsp coconut milk
1 tsp pure vanilla extract

DIRECTIONS

In a small bowl combine 1 tablespoon of ground flaxseeds with 3 tablespoons of water and transfer to the fridge for 15 minutes.

Grease a medium-large mug with a little coconut oil.

In a small bowl combine flour, sugar, cocoa powder, and desiccated coconut.

In a separate bowl combine coconut milk, vanilla extract and flaxseed mixture.

Combine wet and dry ingredients and whisk until a smooth batter is formed.

Microwave on high for around 1 minute and 30 seconds or until the cake has risen and it springs back when you poke it. If it is not fully cooked microwave it for a further 10 seconds until a toothpick comes out clean.

SWEET AVOCADO & COCONUT

Preparation Time
3 minutes

Total Time
4 minutes

Makes
1 serving

INGREDIENTS

4 tbsp all-purpose flour
2 tbsp granulated white sugar
½ tsp baking powder
2 tbsp ripe avocado, mashed
to a puree
3 tbsp dairy free milk
½ tbsp melted coconut oil
1 tbsp desiccated coconut

DIRECTIONS

Grease a medium-large mug with a little coconut or vegetable oil.

In a small bowl combine flour, sugar and baking powder.

In a separate small bowl combine avocado, milk and oil.

Combine the wet and dry ingredients and whisk well until there are no lumps and a smooth batter is formed. Fold in desiccated coconut. Pour into greased mug.

Microwave on high for around 1 minute and 20 seconds or until the cake has risen and it springs back when you poke it. If it is not fully cooked microwave it for a further 10 seconds until a toothpick comes out clean.

MANGO COCONUT CAKE

Preparation Time
3 minutes

Total Time
4 minutes

Makes
1 serving

INGREDIENTS

1 tbsp all-purpose flour
1 tbsp granulated sugar
¼ tsp baking powder
3 tbsp dairy-free milk
1 tbsp desiccated coconut
½ tsp vanilla extract
2 tbsp ripe mangos, cut into
¼-inch chunks

DIRECTIONS

Grease a medium-large mug with a little coconut or vegetable oil.

In a small bowl combine flour, sugar and baking powder.

Add milk, coconut and vanilla and whisk along with the dry ingredients until a smooth batter is formed. Add 1 more tablespoon of milk if the batter seems too dry, however, it needs to be of a thick consistency.

Fold in mango chunks. Pour into greased mug.

Microwave on high for around 1 minute or until the cake has risen and it springs back when you poke it. If it is not fully cooked microwave it for a further 10 seconds until a toothpick comes out clean.

PEAR & ALMOND

Preparation Time
3 minutes
(+ 15 minutes for
flax mixture to set)

Total Time
4 minutes*

Makes
1 serving

INGREDIENTS

1 tbsp ground flax seeds/ chia seeds + 3 tbsp water
2 tbsp coconut flour
1 tbsp almond flour
2 tbsp brown sugar
¼ cup dairy free milk
3 tbsp pears, chopped into ¼-inch chunks

FOR THE TOPPING:

2 tbsp chopped almonds
1 tbsp oats
½ tbsp coconut oil, melted
¼ tsp cinnamon

DIRECTIONS

In a small bowl combine 1 tablespoon of ground flaxseed or chia seeds with 3 tablespoons of water and transfer to the fridge for 15 minutes.

Grease a medium-large mug with a little coconut or vegetable oil.

In a small bowl combine both flours and sugar.

Once the flax/chia mixture has set remove it from the fridge and stir in dairy free milk.

Combine flax mixture with flour mixture and whisk well until there are no lumps and a smooth batter is formed.

Gently fold in pears, then pour into greased mug.

TO MAKE THE TOPPING:

Combine chopped almonds, oats, oil, and cinnamon. Pour on top of mug cake.

Microwave on high for around 90 seconds or until the cake has risen and it springs back when you poke it. If it is not fully cooked microwave it for a further 20 seconds until a toothpick comes out clean.

BANANA NUT CRUNCH

Preparation Time
2 minutes*

Total Time
3 minutes

Makes
1 serving

INGREDIENTS

3 tbsp all-purpose flour
¼ tsp baking powder
Pinch of salt
2 tsp sugar or 1 tbsp maple syrup
1 tbsp + 2 tsp water
1 tbsp soft and ripe mashed banana
½ tsp vanilla extract
Coconut or vegetable oil for greasing

FOR THE TOPPING

¼ tsp cinnamon powder
2 tsp brown sugar
3 tsp mashed banana, (overripe bananas are best)
1 tbsp mixed nuts, toasted & roughly chopped

DIRECTIONS

Grease a medium-large mug with a little coconut or vegetable oil.

In a small bowl combine flour, baking powder, and salt. Add maple syrup/sugar, water, banana and vanilla, and whisk well until a smooth batter is formed. Pour into greased mug and set aside.

In a separate bowl combine all topping ingredients and carefully spoon on top of the cake mixture within the mug.

Microwave on high for around 60 seconds or until the cake has risen and it springs back when you poke it. If it is not fully cooked microwave it for a further 20 seconds until a toothpick comes out clean.

PEANUT BUTTER & BANANA OATMEAL

Preparation Time
2 minutes

Total Time
3 minutes

Makes
1 serving

INGREDIENTS

1 large ripe banana, mashed
2 tbsp peanut butter
½ cup instant oatmeal
Pinch of salt
2 tbsp non-dairy milk
½ tsp ground cinnamon

DIRECTIONS

Grease a medium-large mug with a little oil.

Combine mashed banana with peanut butter. Stir in oatmeal and salt until thoroughly incorporated.

Add 2 tbsp non-dairy milk and mix well.

Pour into the mug and microwave on high for around 2 minutes or until the cake has risen and it springs back when you poke it. If it is not fully cooked microwave it for a further 10 seconds until a toothpick comes out clean.

Sprinkle with ground cinnamon.

PINEAPPLE UPSIDE DOWN MUG CAKE

Preparation Time
2 minutes

Total Time
3 minutes

Makes
1 serving

INGREDIENTS

4 tbsp all purpose flour
2 tbsp + 1 tsp brown sugar, divided
Pinch of salt
¼ tsp baking powder
⅛ tsp baking soda
2 tbsp dairy-free milk

1 tbsp coconut oil, melted
1 tbsp pineapple juice
½ tsp vanilla extract
1 slice pineapple or 2 tbsp pineapple chunks, canned or fresh

DIRECTIONS

Grease a medium-large mug with a little coconut oil and sprinkle the booth with 1 teaspoon of brown sugar.

In a small bowl combine flour, sugar, salt, baking powder, and baking soda.

In a separate bowl combine milk, oil, pineapple juice and vanilla extract and stir.

Combine wet and dry ingredients and whisk until a smooth batter is formed.

Place pineapple slice or chunks into the bottom of the mug then pour in batter.

Microwave on high for around 1 minute and 30 seconds or until the cake has risen and it springs back when you poke it. If it is not fully cooked microwave it for a further 10 seconds until a toothpick comes out clean.

Leave to cool for 5 minutes then use a knife around the edge of the mug to release the cake and tip upside down on a plate.

RASPBERRY ALMOND CAKE

Preparation Time
3 minutes
(+15 minutes for
the flax egg to set)

Total Time
4 minutes

Makes
1 serving

INGREDIENTS

1 tbsp ground flax seeds + 3 tbsp water
1 tbsp maple syrup
3 tbsp non-dairy milk
1 tsp vanilla extract
4 level tbsp almond flour
½ tsp baking powder
1 tbsp vegan butter, melted
7 fresh raspberries
1 tbsp almonds, chopped

DIRECTIONS

In a small microwaveable bowl melt butter for about 10-20 seconds.

Combine the flax seeds and water in a bowl and leave in fridge to set for 15 minutes

Grease a medium-large mug with a little oil.

Combine maple syrup, milk and vanilla. Slowly add flour, baking powder and the flax mixture- whisking well after each addition. Finally, add melted butter.

Fold in raspberries and almonds.

Pour into the mug and microwave on high for 1 minute and 30 seconds or until the cake has risen and it springs back when you poke it. If it is not fully cooked microwave it for a further 10 seconds until a toothpick comes out clean.

SPICED SWEET POTATO MUG CAKE

Preparation Time
2 minutes
(+15 minutes for
the flax/chia egg
to set)

Total Time
4 minutes

Makes
1 serving

INGREDIENTS

1 tbsp ground flax seeds /
chia seeds + 3 tbsp water
2 tbsp cooked & mashed
sweet potato (skin removed
and mashed to a puree)
2 tbsp dairy free milk
1 tbsp water
½ tsp vanilla extract
3 tbsp all purpose flour

¼ tsp baking powder
1 tbsp brown sugar
Pinch of salt
¼ tsp ground cinnamon
¼ tsp ground nutmeg
½ tsp ground ginger
1 ½ tbsp roasted walnuts,
chopped

DIRECTIONS

In a small bowl combine 1 tablespoon of ground flaxseed or chia seeds with 3 tablespoons of water and transfer to the fridge for 15 minutes.

Grease a medium-large mug with a little coconut oil.

In a small bowl combine sweet potato, milk, water and vanilla.

In a separate bowl combine flour, baking powder, sugar, salt, cinnamon, nutmeg, and ginger.

Combine wet and dry ingredients and whisk until a smooth batter is formed then stir in flaxseed mixture. Fold in chopped hazelnuts then pour into the mug.

Microwave on high for around 1 minute and 30 seconds or until the cake has risen and it springs back when you poke it. If it is not fully cooked microwave it for a further 10 seconds until a toothpick comes out clean.

LEMON MUG CAKE WITH LEMON DRIZZLE

Preparation Time
2 minutes

Total Time
5 minutes

Makes
1 cup

INGREDIENTS

FOR THE MUG CAKE:

1 tbsp freshly squeezed lemon juice
2 tsp lemon zest
2 tbsp non-dairy milk
1 tbsp melted coconut oil
1 tsp vanilla extract
3 tbsp all purpose flour

¼ tsp baking powder
2 tbsp sugar
Pinch of salt

FOR THE LEMON DRIZZLE:

3 tbsp confectioners sugar
3 tbsp freshly squeezed lemon juice
1 tsp lemon zest

DIRECTIONS

Grease a medium-large mug with a little coconut oil.

In a small bowl combine lemon juice, lemon zest, milk, oil, and vanilla.

In a separate bowl combine flour, baking powder, sugar, and salt.

Combine wet and dry ingredients and whisk until a smooth batter is formed. Set aside while you make the lemon drizzle.

TO MAKE THE LEMON DRIZZLE:

Combine sugar and lemon juice. Add 1 tbsp of water at a time and continue to stir until the drizzle is of a thick but smooth consistency.

Add the lemon zest and mix well.

Once the glaze is ready, microwave the mug cake on high for around 1 minute and 30 seconds or until the cake has risen and it springs back when you poke it. If it is not fully cooked microwave it for a further 10 seconds until a toothpick comes out clean. Cool for 2-3 minutes before glazing.

Use a tablespoon to drizzle over mug cakes.

TOPPINGS

SALTED CARAMEL SAUCE

Preparation Time
5 minutes
(+4 hour for
cashew nuts to
soak)

Total Time
15 minutes

Makes
2 servings

INGREDIENTS

2 tbsp + 2 tsp non-dairy milk (
6 tbsp water, divided
⅓ cup raw cashews (soaked in boiling water for 4 hours or
overnight)
⅓ cup white sugar
1 tbsp coconut oil
½ tsp coarse salt
1 tsp vanilla extract

DIRECTIONS

In a blender or food processor mix milk, 3 tbsp water and
cashew nuts until completely smooth, pulse for around 2-3
minutes on high speed.

In a large saucepan heat sugar and 3 tbsp water until sugar
has dissolved. Bring to a boil but do not stir! You can swirl the
caramel around the pan to prevent the edges burning.

The syrup is ready once it starts to turn light golden brown,
around 5-6 minutes. If it has turned amber you may need to
make another batch as it is likely to have burned.

Remove from the heat and whisk in coconut oil and vanilla
extract. Slowly add milk/cashew nut mixture. Do not worry if it
vigorously bubbles, this is normal.

Continue to whisk over a low heat until the mixture is smooth.

Stir in coarse salt then remove from the heat and set aside.

Wait at least 10 minutes for the caramel sauce to cool down before serving.

CHOCOLATE CHIPS

Preparation Time
10 minutes

Total Time
10 minutes
(+ 60 minutes to
chill)

Makes approx.
½ cup chocolate
chips

INGREDIENTS

¼ cup cacao butter
¼ cup unsweetened cocoa powder
1 tbsp maple syrup

DIRECTIONS

In a medium saucepan heat 2-3 inches of water over medium heat but do not bring to a boil. Set a small bowl gently onto the water, making sure not to get any liquid inside the bowl and place cacao butter or coconut oil inside.

Once fully melted remove from heat, add cocoa powder and maple syrup, and whisk til smooth.

Lay the honeycomb mould over a piece of baking paper or foil to catch any spills, and using a spoon slowly and gently pour the chocolate sauce, filling each hole.

Using the baking paper or foil for stability, transfer to the freezer to chill for 60 minutes.

Remove from freezer and pop all the chocolate chips out over a bowl.

Store the chocolate chips in a freezer bag and leave in the fridge or freezer as they will soften at room temperature.

COCONUT CREAM TOPPING

Preparation Time
2 minutes
(+ 4 hour for
cashews to soak)

Total Time
5 minutes

Makes approx.
2 servings

INGREDIENTS

2 tbsp cashews, soaked in water for 4 hour
2 tsp coconut butter or cacao butter
1 tsp sugar
Pinch of coarse salt

DIRECTIONS

Drain the cashew nuts and-and pat dry, then whip with coconut butter, salt, and sugar.

Continue to whip by hand or in a stand mixer until smooth and fluffy.

PREVIEW OF 'THE ESSENTIAL MEXICAN COOKBOOK FOR VEGANS' INCLUDING A FREE RECIPE!

From Fully Loaded Nachos and Wedges with Vegan Nacho Cheese to Sweet Mexican Rice Milk and Crispy Mexican Churros, this cookbook celebrates the flavors of Mexico and shows you how easy it is to prepare authentic and delicious vegan dishes in your very own kitchen - on even the busiest of weeknights.

Mexican food has become increasingly popular throughout the Western world where you will see Mexican restaurants popping up on your local high street and ready made Mexican meals on the supermarket shelves. Traditional Mexican cuisine is a fusion of the ancient Aztec and Mayan Indians with ingredients and cooking techniques that originated from all over the world including Spanish and Indian influences.

The basic staples of this cuisine come in the form of simple, easy to source, natural ingredients such as corn, pulses and rice - making it very easy to adapt the recipes to the vegan diet.

Our philosophy is to bring an authentic Mexican street food flavor to vegans all over the world and to enable you to enjoy veganised versions of your favorite meals such as Fajitas, Burritos and Chili, along with delicious desserts including Churros and Chili Chocolate Avocado Mousse.

The recipes have been carefully tried, tested and refined to retain an authentic taste and texture, yet uses simple and straight-forward ingredients found in your local supermarket. The emphasis is on cooking traditional, authentically flavored dishes for even the most inexperienced of cooks, making your life simpler and your meal preparation easier.

Whether you are a vegan, vegetarian or meat-eater looking to reduce the amount of animal produce in your diet, the 'Love Vegan' series of cookbooks will inspire you to cook delicious authentically flavored Mexican vegan dishes on even the busiest of weeknights.

AVOCADO ENCHILADAS

These mouthwatering vegan black bean & avocado enchiladas are stuffed with fresh ingredients and smothered in a homemade enchilada sauce for an authentic Mexican experience, any night of the week.

Preparation Time
15 minutes

Total Time
45 minutes

Makes
6 enchiladas

INGREDIENTS

2 tbsp olive or vegetable oil
2 medium garlic cloves, finely chopped
1 white onion, sliced
1 red bell pepper, sliced
1 (420g) can black beans, drained and rinsed
1 (420g) can chickpeas, drained and rinsed
2 large avocados, peeled, pitted and chopped
⅓ cup nutritional yeast
3 medium tomatoes, chopped
2 tsp cumin powder
1 tsp paprika
½ tsp cayenne pepper
½ tsp salt
¼ tsp pepper

6 large tortillas

FOR THE ENCHILADA SAUCE:

2 tbsp olive or vegetable oil
3 cups vegetable stock
¼ cup tomato puree
¼ cup all-purpose flour
2 tbsp olive oil
2 tsp cumin powder
½ tsp chili powder
¼ tsp garlic powder
¼ tsp onion powder
½ tsp dried oregano
½ tsp coarse salt
½ tsp freshly ground black pepper

DIRECTIONS

Heat a large frying pan with oil over medium heat. Once hot add onions and peppers and saute for 4-5 minutes until soft. Add garlic and fry for 1-2 minutes.

Reduce heat to low and add cumin, paprika and cayenne, stirring constantly for 30 seconds until the spices are fragrant.

Add the chopped tomatoes, avocado, nutritional yeast, black band and chickpeas and mix well. Heat for 5-6 minutes then remove from heat and set aside.

Next prepare the enchilada sauce. In a small bowl combine flour, cumin, chili, garlic, onion and oregano.

Heat a frying pan with oil over medium heat. Once hot add the tomato paste and fry, moving it around frequently for 30 seconds. Slowly add the flour and spice mixture and mix well to combine. Cook for 30 seconds to 1 minutes using a whisk to stir constantly.

Pour in the vegetable stock and bring mixture to a boil, then reduce heat and simmer for 8-10 minutes until the sauce has thickened and reduced.

Preheat the oven to 175° and grease a 9x13 inch oven dish with a little oil.

Place tortilla wraps on a clean surface and evenly distribute bean mixture between the 6 wraps, rolling each one tightly and tuck in the ends then transfer to the greased oven dish.

Pour over the enchilada sauce, covering each wrap and bake for 25 minutes.

Serve immediately while hot.

MORE GREAT TITLES

• •

HIGH CEDAR PRESS

CHECK OUT THE FULL COLLECTION!

Printed in Great Britain
by Amazon